RASPBERRY PI3 GUIDE FOR BEGINNERS

By Steven Giles

The trademarks that are used are without any consent, and the publication of the trademark is without permission or backing by the trademark owner. All trademarks and brands within this book are for clarifying purposes only and are the owned by the owners themselves, not affiliated with this document.

Disclaimer and Terms of Use: The Author and Publisher has strived to be as accurate and complete as possible in the creation of this book, notwithstanding the fact that he does not warrant or represent at any time that the contents within are accurate due to the rapidly changing nature of the Internet. While all attempts have been made to verify information provided in this publication, the Author and Publisher assumes no responsibility for errors, omissions, or contrary interpretation of the subject matter herein.

Any perceived slights of specific persons, peoples, or organizations are unintentional. In practical advice books, like anything else in life, there are no guarantees of results. Readers are cautioned to rely on their own judgment about their individual circumstances and act accordingly.

This book is not intended for use as a source of legal, medical, business, accounting or financial advice. All readers are advised to seek services of competent professionals in the legal, medical, business, accounting, and finance fields.

TABLE OF CONTENTS

INTRODUCTION

This book explores a number of things you can do with your Raspberry Pi 3, from controlling hardware with Python, to using it as a media centre, or building games in Scratch. The beauty of the Raspberry Pi 3 is that it's just a very tiny general purpose computer (which may be a little slower than you're used to for some desktop applications, but much better at some other stuff than a regular PC), so you can do anything you could do on a regular computer with it. In addition, the Raspberry Pi3 has powerful multimedia and 3D graphics capabilities, so it has the potential to be used as a games platform, and we very much hope to see people starting to write games for it.

We think physical computing building systems using sensors, motors, lights and micro controllers is something that gets overlooked in favour of pure software projects in a lot of instances, and it's a shame, because physical computing is massive fun. To the extent that there's any children's computing movement at the moment, it's a physical computing movement. The LOGO turtles that represented physical computing when we were kids are now fighting robots, quadcopters or parentsensing bedroom doors, and we love it. However, the lack of General Purpose Input/Output (GPIO) on home PCs is a real handicap for many people getting started with robotics projects. The Raspberry Pi 3 exposes GPIO so you can get to work straight away.

I keep being surprised by ideas the community comes up with which wouldn't have crossed my mind in a thousand years: the Australian school meteortracking project; the Boreatton Scouts in the UK and their robot, which is controlled via an electron cephalography headset (the world's first robot controlled by Scouting brainwaves); the family who are building a robot vacuum cleaner. And I'm a real space cadet, so reading about the people sending Raspberry Pi 3s into near earth orbit on rockets and balloons gives me goose bumps.

Success for us would be another 1,000 people every year taking up Computer Science at the university level in the UK. That would not only be beneficial for the country, the software and hardware industries, and the economy; but it would be even more beneficial for every one of those 1,000 people, who, I hope, discover that there's a whole world of possibilities and a great deal of fun to be had out there. Building a robot when you're a kid can take you to places you never imagined I know because it happened to me!

When the Raspberry Pi 3 was out, I was very eager to get one. But to be on a safer side I made a detailed study and came up with the best combination of accessories which helped me to have a hassle free experience with the latest model.

The aim of this instructable is to provide a complete guide to beginners on selection of suitable accessories and the Operating systems compatible with Raspberry Pi 3.

CHAPTER I:
RASPBERRY PI 3

The Raspberry Pi3 is a wonderful microcomputer that brims with potential. With a Raspberry Pi3 you can build robots, learn to code, and create all kinds of weird and wonderful projects. Hackers and enthusiasts have turned Raspberry Pi3 boards into fully automated weather stations, internet connected beehives, motorised skateboards, and much more. The only limit is your imagination.

But first, you need to start at the beginning. Upon picking up your Raspberry Pi3 for the first time, you're faced with a small green board of chips and sockets and may have no idea what to do with it. Before you can start building the project of your dreams, you'll need to get the basics sorted: keyboard, mouse, display, and operating system.

The Raspberry Pi3 is the ultimate, affordable computer for anyone who likes to tinker and doesn't mind doing some legwork to get it up and running.

Creating projects with a Raspberry Pi3 is fun once you've mastered the basics. So in this guide, we're going to take you from newbie zero to Raspberry Pi3 hero. Grab your Raspberry Pi3 and let's get going.

Raspberry Pi 3 is packed in a small white cardboard box as usual. What you get when you open up the box is just the credit card sized board with a Safety Guide and a Quick Start Guide printed in different languages. You can not do anything with the board unless you combine other accessories mentioned in the next step.

CHAPTER 2:
DOWNLOADING AND
INSTALLING RASPBERRY PI

Raspbian is the Foundation's official supported Operating System. NOOBS is the built-in operating system installer for Raspberry Pi. But if you already know which operating system you want to use, there's a quicker way to get your Pi up and running.

The Raspberry Pi is the ultimate, affordable computer for anyone who likes to tinker and doesn't mind doing some legwork to get it up and running.

If you order a Raspberry Pi without an SD card preloaded with New Out Of Box Software (NOOBS), you will need to provide your own SD card and manually install an operating system.

There are many to choose from like Raspbian or OSMC for media streaming and they're all quick and easy to install. There are even operating systems that turn your Raspberry Pi into a music streamer.

HERE'S HOW TO INSTALL (AKA "FLASH") AN OS TO THE RASPBERRY PI WITHOUT NOOBS.

WHAT YOU'LL NEED

Begin by downloading the software that you want to install on the Raspberry Pi. In this case, we're using Raspbian, a Raspberry Pioptimized version of the Linux distribution called Debian, which you can find by going to raspberrypi.org/downloads. Click Raspbian (instead of NOOBS) and download the full Raspbian

Jessie ZIP. The file is approximately 1.3GB, so it may take several minutes to download, depending on your internet speeds.

You'll also need a freshlyformatted SD card (microSD cards are required for the Raspberry Pi 2 or 3). The format used by Raspberry Pi is FAT32 (or MSDOS), not exFAT. If you have an SD card larger than 32GB, make sure it is using the proper format, as anything larger than 32GB defaults to exFAT.

To do this on a Mac, open Disk Utility, select the drive you want to format, click Erase. Choose MSDOS (FAT) for the format and click Erase.

On Windows, it's recommended that you use the SD Association's Formatting Tool, which is available free of charge at sdcard.org. Open SDFormatter and, according to Raspberry Pi Foundation, you "need to set FORMAT SIZE ADJUSTMENT option to ON" in the program's settings to ensure you format the entire SD card.

INSTALLING RASPBIAN WITH MAC OR WINDOWS

To install Raspbian, you will need to write the operating system image file onto the SD card.

Debian with Raspberry Pi Desktop is the Foundation's operating system for PC and Mac. You can create a live disc, run it in a virtual machine, or even install it on your computer.

Start by uncompressing the ZIP file you downloaded from raspberrypi.org. To do this from a Mac, install The Unarchiver and double-click the ZIP file. From Windows, right-click the file, select Extract All, choose a destination for the extracted files and click Extract. After it's done unzipping, it's time to write the image.

MAC

Open Terminal by locating the app in Launchpad or by pressing command + spacebar and searching for the app in Spotlight.

Change the directory you're working in to the location of the extracted image. For example, if you extracted the Raspbian image to your desktop, type cd Desktop/ and press enter.

Identify the disk by typing diskutil list and pressing enter. Look for the name of the SD card you're using (it will appear the same in Terminal as it does on the desktop) and locate its identifier, which will look something like disk2 or disk3, depending on how many devices you have connected to your Mac.

Make sure you have the right storage device identifier and type the command diskutil unmountDisk /dev/[disk identifier] and press return. The command should look something like diskutil unmountDisk /dev/disk2.

Finally, write the image to the disk using the command sudo dd bs=1m if=[image]. img of=/dev/r[disk identifier] and press return. The complete command will look something like sudo dd bs=1m if=20160318raspbianjessie.img of=/dev/ rdisk2. You will need to enter the administrator password to your computer and press enter once more.

WINDOWS

The process for Windows is a bit more straightforward. You will first need to download Win32 Disk Imager from SourceForge.

Once Win32 Disk Imager is installed, run it as an administrator by right-clicking the program icon and selecting Run as administrator.

Select the image file you extracted from the Raspbian ZIP file.

Select the correct storage drive by choosing the drive letter in the dropdown menu below Device. Be completely certain you selected the correct drive before proceeding.

Click Write.

This process will take several minutes to complete, but once the image is finished writing to the SD card, you can eject the drive, insert it into the Raspberry Pi and power it on.

The first boot will take longer than usual, but you will have a working version of Raspbian installed.

CHAPTER 3:
SETTING UP THE RASPBERRY PI 3

B efore getting to the amazing part, however, you must first set up that tiny computer in your hand. Don't worry because I'm here for those who need more guidance on that journey.

You probably want to get started with learning to code or building cool new things right away but there are a few things you need to take care of before jumping into that and the two most important things are equipment and an Operating System. Other than those, the Raspberry Pi 3 is already a complete computer system at a really affordable price.

Just like most toys with a "Batteries not included" note on their packaging, the credit card sized Raspberry Pi 3 does not come with the tools you need to make it run so you first have to ensure that you have the correct cables, external memory, and peripherals to be able to use it.

WHAT YOU WILL NEED

Despite the Pi 3's small size, it has enough ports to attach necessary cables and peripherals and is Wifi and Bluetooth enabled for a comfortable user experience. It has four USB 2.0 ports and an HDMI output, which means USB hubs are not really needed for basic use. It is also powered through a microUSB port, much like smartphones.

BASICALLY, WHAT YOU WILL NEED TO HOOK UP TO THE PI 3 ARE THE FOLLOWING:

- HDMI monitor*

- USB mouse

- USB keyboard

- microSD card with a minimum capacity of 8GB and a card reader

- 2A (2,000 mAh) microUSB power supply, charger or adapter

*For the HDMI monitor, you can use an HDMI television or any monitor with an HDMI input port.

Connect!

Assuming that you have all the equipment you need, start connecting the cables to your Pi 3. Take note, however, that you should connect and plugin the power supply last for obvious reasons.

But if it is not obvious enough, we are talking about electricity. Just like with any setup that involves electricity, power already begins to course through one the device is plugged in so it is better to be safe than electrocuted.

VERIFY YOUR VERSION

Some Raspberry Pi Model 3 versions already have the latest Raspbian OS installed while others do not. If you're one of the lucky people to have been given a Pi 3 with a preinstalled Raspbian OS, you can head on straight to the Raspberry Pi Organization's website and look up several cool projects from both the team and the community of fellow users. If there is no OS, however, please read on.

SET UP RASPBIAN OS

Assuming that you have got everything connected and powered up, you can start following the steps below to get you started.

Step 1: Download the latest Raspbian OS

This is where the microSD and card reader comes in because the Raspbian OS, which is over 4GB, will have to be installed in it. Unlike the typical computer setup, the Pi 3 does not have the luxury of an internal memory so both the system and the user must rely on a good, not easily corruptible microSD in its stead.

You can download the latest Raspbian OS here and manually install the image but beginners should opt to install via New Out of Box Software (NOOBS) instead. If you choose to install manually, skip to step 4. If you choose NOOBS, continue to step 2.

Step 2: Format the microSD card as FAT

Assuming you chose to use NOOBS to install Raspbian, you will also have to prepare the microSD card by formatting it as FAT32a necessary step for NOOBS. But don't worry, doing that is easy. All you have to do is download and use the SD Association's SD Card Formatter and ensure that the "Format Size Adjustment" optionin the Options Menu is turned ON and you're good to go.

The SD Card Formatter is also available for Mac users but with additional instructions and Linux users can use gparted. You can find additional instructions here.

Step 3: Extract NOOBS

The Raspberry Pi Organization offers NOOBS and NOOBS Lite in its website for easier OS installation. However, do note that what you need is NOOBS because the Lite version does not have the latest Raspbian OS preinstalled, so save yourself the time, hassle, and frustration.

Use 7Zip for Windows or The Unarchiver for Mac to extract the files you need. Note that the two unzip tools are not required, however, they are also the ones which proved to correctly unzip the necessary files without corrupting any of the files contained in the archive.

Once this is successfully done, copy all the extracted files onto the microSD card then insert it in the card reader the insert that in an available USB port.

Step 4: Hook up and set up

Make sure the connections are all secure to the display and peripherals are all secure then power up your Pi 3. Now wait a bit while NOOBS boots up and prepares your Pi 3.

When the loading process is complete, you will see a window asking you to install an operating system and you just have to choose Raspbian and your default language and NOOBS will do the rest. Once the installation is complete, NOOBS will restart your Pi 3 and it will now boot up with the Raspbian OS desktop where you can configure everything else.

Step 5: Personalize it

Once the desktop is booted up, it will now be easier for you to access your WiFi and pair Bluetooth devices or peripherals. Play around with your new system and look up some projects you can do.

ANOTHER WAY FOR A HEADLESS RASPBERRY PI

In the event that you have no extra HDMI television or display monitors on hand, you can still install the Raspbian by connecting to it using another laptop or desktop.

The Raspberry Pi Organization has outlined instructions on installing the Raspbian via a Secure Shell (SSH) for Linux or Mac or Remote Access so take a look at it if you can't wait to use your Pi 3.

CHAPTER 4:
USING RASPBERRY PI3

You could create a dedicated gaming device, or an external storage box for movies and music. There are a plethora of Raspberry Pi3 projects that cover all manner of possibilities, each one with different specifications. We have a guide for getting started with Raspberry Pi3 to help you understand what you will need for your first (or next) project.

WHAT YOU WILL NEED

The Raspberry Pi3 ships as just the singleboard mini computer. There are a few additional components you will need before you can get started. So, when making your purchase, keep in mind that you'll need the following extras.

1. RASPBERRY PI

There are five different models of Raspberry Pi. The Pi 2 Model B or Pi 1 Model B+ and Pi 3 Model B are ideal for beginner projects because they are the most versatile and have the widest range of capabilities. The Pi 3 Model B has the added bonus of having a quadcore processor and 1 GB of RAM so it supports heavier operating systems, like Ubuntu and Microsoft 10. The Model A+ is a powerful board for building robotics, but doesn't have an Ethernet port and only comes with one USB port. So, it's better for people that are a little more savvy with engineering technology. Raspberry Pi Zero is basically a miniature version of the Model A+, but has a more robust computing power. It has a micro USB port and mini HDMI port for 1080p output compatibility, but doesn't have wireless capability. It only costs $5, but unfortunately, it is super hard to find and you're going to see inflated pricing for it. CanaKit still has a starter kit available, which is worth the extra money because it comes with everything you need to get started with Raspberry Pi3.

2. POWER SUPPLY.

You will need a 5V microUSB power supply. You can find them for really cheap online. You may even have one from a nonapple mobile device lying around the house. I recommend the CanaKit 5V power supply.

3. USB KEYBOARD

4. USB MOUSE.

If you prefer to use a Bluetooth keyboard and mouse, you could just get a Bluetooth adapter. I have a Kinivo BTD400, but there are dozens of different brands out there.

5. MICROSD CARD.

The microSD card must have at least 8 GB of storage. You can purchase one that comes preloaded with Raspberry Pi's New Out of Box Software (NOOBS), but you can also download the software for free from the website, so there is no need to purchase a special NOOBS microSD card.

6. MICROSD USB CARD READER.

You'll need something that you can connect the microSD card to your PC or Mac in order to download software onto it. Adafruit carries one that is perfect for Raspberry Pi, but you can pick one up at just about any electronics or office supply store.

7. A MONITOR OR TV THAT SUPPORTS HDMI OR COMPOSITE VIDEO.

You can use an older composite video display, but HDMI works better and supports audio transfers.

8. AN HDMI CABLE OR COMPOSITE VIDEO CABLE

An HDMI cable or composite video cable, depending on what the screen you use supports.

9. AN ETHERNET CABLE (OR WIFI DONGLE).

A connection to the Internet is not required for setup, but many Raspberry Pi projects use them.

CHAPTER 5:
RASPBERRY PI3 BASIC

SYSTEM ON CHIP (SOC)

WHAT IS SYSTEM ON CHIP?
-   A complex IC that integrates the major functional elements into a single chip or chipset.

*   programmable processor

*   onchip memory

*   accelerating function hardware (e.g. GPU)

*   both hardware and software

*   analog components

BENEFITS OF SOC
-   Reduce overall system cost
-   Increase performance
-   Lower power consumption
-   Reduce size
-   BCM2835 SoC Multimedia processor

CPU

- ARM 1176JZFS (armv6k) 700MHz
- RISC Architecture and low power draw
- Not compatible with traditional PC software

GPU

- Broadcom Video IV
- Specialized graphical instruction sets

RAM

- 512MB (Model B rev.2)
- 256 MB (Model A, Model B rev.1)

CONNECTING A DISPLAY AND AUDIO

HDMI

- Digital signal
- Video and audio signal
- DVI cannot carry audio signal
- Up to 1920x1200 resolution

COMPOSITE RCA

- Analog signal
- 480i, 576i resolution

3.5MM JACK

RPi Remote Connections

http://pihw.wordpress.com/guides/directnetworkconnection/

UNIVERSAL SERIAL BUS

- Two USB 2.0 ports in RPi

- Buy a powered USB hub

Passive models are cheaper and smaller, but lack the ability to run current hungry devices like CD drives and external hard drives.

Storage: Secure Digital (SD)

FORM FACTOR
- SD, Mini SD, Micro SD

TYPES OF CARD
- SDSC (SD): 1MB to 2GB
- SDHC: 4GB to 32 GB
- SDXD up to 2TB

The card should be at least 2GB in capacity to store all the required files Storage:

CONTINUE SD FORMATTER:

https://www.sdcard.org/downloads/formatter_4/

HOW TO MOUNT USB FLASH DRIVE FROM COMMAND LINE:

http://linuxcommando.blogspot.co.uk/2007/12/howtomountusbflashdrivefrom.html

NETWORKING WIRELESS

IEEE 802.11 WIFI
- **Protocols**

- 802.11 b, up to 11Mbps

- 802.11 g, up to 54Mbps

- 802.11 n, up to 300Mbps

- 802.11 ac (draft), up to
  - 1Gbps
  - Frequency band

- 2.4GHz, 5GHz

LOW SPEED PERIPHERALS

- General Purpose

INPUT/OUTPUT (GPIO)
- Pins can be configured to be input/output
- Reading from various environmental sensors

- Ex: IR, video, temperature, 3axis orientation, acceleration
  - Writing output to dc motors, LEDs for status.

POWER CONSUMPTION

- microUSB power connector
  - 2.5W (model A)
  - 3.5W (model B)

- Powered USB hub
  - To provide more power for USB peripherals

USEFUL LINKS

- Raspberry Pi official website
  - *http://www.raspberrypi.org/*

- Raspberry Pi wiki
  - *http://elinux.org/RaspberryPiBoard*

- Raspberry Pi verified peripherals
  - *http://elinux.org/RPi_VerifiedPeripherals*

- The MagPi
  - *http://www.themagpi.com*

- Raspberry Pi on Adafruit Learning System:
  - *http://learn.adafruit.com/category/learnraspberrypi*

REMAPPING KEYBOARD:

- sudo vi /etc/default/keyboard

  XKBLAYOUT="gb"

  Change "gb" to "us"

- (This assumes you want a us mapping, if not replace the gb with the two letter code for your country)

INSTALL AND START SSH

- Update aptget package index files:
  - sudo aptget update

- Install SSH:
  - sudo aptget install ssh

- Start SSH server:
  - sudo /etc/init.d/ssh start

- To start the SSH server every time the Pi boots up:
  - sudo updaterc.d ssh defaults

- SSH client for Windows:
  - PuTTY
  - *http://www.putty.org/*

- SSH Secure File Transfer
  - *http://www.utexas.edu/learn/upload/ssh_client.html*

INSTALL JAVA

- 1. JDK 8 (with JavaFX) for ARM Early Access
  http://jdk8.java.net/fxarmpreview/
  - Download from Raspberry pi
  - Download from your own PC and copy it (scp) to

RASPBERRY PI

- Extract the JDK tar.gz file
  - tar –zxvf fileToExtract.tar.gz
  - You will get a folder "jdk1.8.0"

SET JAVA PATH

- If you put the folder "jdk1.8.0" in the home directory (i.e. /home/pi), you will see the java executables (e.g. javac, java, appletviewer) in the directory: /home/pi/jdk1.8.0/bin

- open /etc/profile add:

  PATH=$PATH:/home/pi/jdk1.8.0/bin export PATH

- Reboot:

  sudo reboot

SOFTWARE

- LXTerminal and Root Terminal: use the Linux command line in a window without leaving the GUI.

- Midori & NetSurf: Lightweight web browser

- IDLE and IDLE 3: IDE for Python 2.7 and 3

- Task Manager: Checks the available memory, processor workload, closes crashed or unresponsive programs

- Music player at the console: moc

- OpenOffice.org: sudo aptget install openoffice.org

- Image Editing: Gimp

- LAMP (Linux, Apache, MySQL and PHP) stack

- Sudo aptget install apache2 php5 php5mysql mysqlserver

INSTALLING, UNINSTALLING AND UPDATING SOFTWARE

- Package manager in Debian: apt

- GUI for apt, Synaptic Package Manager doesn't work well on Pi due to the lack of memory

- Make sure that the apt cache is up to date:

- aptget update

- Finding software:

- aptcache search emacs

- Installing software and dependencies:

- sudo aptget install emacs

- Uninstalling software:

- sudo aptget remove emacs

- sudo aptget purge emacs (removes everything including configurations)

- Upgrading software:

- Sudo aptget upgrade

- Sudo aptget install emacs

TROUBLESHOOTING

Keyboard and Mouse Diagnostics

Power Diagnostics

Display Diagnostics

Network Diagnostics

Emergency Kernel

WIRED NETWORKING CONFIGURATION

sudo nano /etc/ntework/interfaces

iface eth0 inet static

[tab] address 192.168.0.10

[tab] netmask 255.255.255.0

[tab] gateway 192.168.0.254

sudo /etc/init.d/networking restart

sudo nano /etc/reslov.conf

nameserver 8.8.8.8

nameserver 8.8.4.4

sudo /etc/init.d/networking restart

ping –c 1 www.raspberrypi.org

WIRELESS NETWORKING CONFIGURATION

- USB WiFi adapters are very powerhungry. Connect a powered USB hub to the Pi, and then insert the WiFi adapter into that.

- Print out the entire kernel ring buffer and find out the company that makes the actual chip: mesg | grep ^usb
  - Atmelfirmware
  - Firmwareatheros
  - Firmwarebrcm80211
  - Firmewareintelwimax
  - Firmwareipw2x00
  - Firmwareiwlwifi
  - Firmwareralink
  - Firmwarerealteck
  - Zd1211firmware

- Check the current status of the network: iwconfig

CHAPTER 6: INSTALLING WINDOWS ON A RASPBERRY PI3

TO GET UP AND RUNNING YOU NEED A FEW BITS AND PIECES:

Raspberry Pi 3. 5V 2A microUSB power supply. 8GB or larger Class 10 microSD card with fullsize SD adapter. HDMI cable. Access to a PC. USB WiFi adapter (older models of Raspberry Pi) or Ethernet cable.

At this point, the HDMI cable is only to plug the Raspberry Pi into a display so you can make sure your install worked. Some Raspberry Pi starter kits include everything you need, but the list above covers the power, display, and something to install Windows 10 IoT Core on.

HOW TO INSTALL WINDOWS 10 IOT ON THE RASPBERRY PI 3

For the first part, you don't need the Raspberry Pi at all, just the microSD card in its adapter and your PC. A prerequisite is that you're running Windows 10 version 10.0.10240 or higher.

Go to the Windows 10 developer center.

Click Get Windows 10 IoT Core Dashboard to download the necessary application.

Install the application and open it. Select set up a new device from the sidebar.

Select the options as shown in the image below. Make sure you select the correct drive for your microSD card and give your device a name and admin password.

Select the WiFi network connection you want your Raspberry Pi to connect to, if required. Only networks your PC connects to will be shown. Click download and install.

The application will now download the necessary files from Microsoft and flash them to your microSD card. It'll take a little while, but the dashboard will show you the progress.

Once the image has been installed to the microSD card, it's time to eject it from your PC and go over to the Raspberry Pi. First connect up the microUSB cable and power supply, HDMI cable and USB WiFi adapter or Ethernet cable. Connect the HDMI cable to your chosen display, insert the microSD card into the Raspberry Pi and power it up.

SETTING UP

Unlike "proper" Windows 10, there's not much of a setup process here. You'll be asked to choose a language and enter your WiFi password to connect to the web. That's about it. It'll take a couple of minutes, but when booted up you'll see the Windows 10 IoT Core splash screen.

It's deliberately light and you don't have access to much. The Windows 10 part is designed to disappear, as once you deploy an app to your Raspberry Pi, it becomes that app. There's no flipping in and out of Windows and launching apps like you would on a PC.

When booted, you can go back to the dashboard application on your PC, and you'll see your Raspberry Pi listed as one of your devices.

To get a feel for how things operate you can deploy a selection of sample applications to your Raspberry Pi to see how Windows disappears, and all you're left with is the application designed to run on the IoT Core. These include the classic Hello World, an Internet Radio app and something to network connect a 3D printer.

Developing is much more complex, but at least if you're interested in this new branch of Windows 10, it's easy and cheap to get up and running. To go further you'll need to download Visual Studio and start building code. Microsoft has a whole bundle of resources at your disposal, however, to help you get the most from your Windows 10 IoT Core experience.

CHAPTER 7:
RASPBIAN

Raspbian is a free operating system based on Debian optimized for the Raspberry Pi hardware. An operating system is the set of basic programs and utilities that make your Raspberry Pi run. However, Raspbian provides more than a pure OS: it comes with over 35,000 packages, precompiled software bundled in a nice format for easy installation on your Raspberry Pi.

The initial build of over 35,000 Raspbian packages, optimized for best performance on the Raspberry Pi, was completed in June of 2012. However, Raspbian is still under active development with an emphasis on improving the stability and performance of as many Debian packages as possible.

Note: Raspbian is not affiliated with the Raspberry Pi Foundation. Raspbian was created by a small, dedicated team of developers that are fans of the Raspberry Pi hardware, the educational goals of the Raspberry Pi Foundation and, of course, the Debian Project.

Raspbian comes preinstalled with plenty of software for education, programming and general use. It has Python, Scratch, Sonic Pi, Java, Mathematica and more.

The Raspbian with Desktop image contained in the ZIP archive is over 4GB in size, which means that these archives use features which are not supported by older unzip tools on some platforms. If you find that the download appears to be corrupt or the file is not unzipping correctly, please try using 7Zip (Windows) or The Unarchiver (Macintosh). Both are free of charge and have been tested to unzip the image correctly.

SUPPORT RASPBIAN

Raspbian is a community funded and supported free software effort. Although Raspbian is free software, the development costs associated with it are not free.

CHAPTER 8: USING PYTHON ON YOUR RASPBERRY PI3

WHAT IS A PYTHON PROGRAM?

Python is a very useful programming language that has an easy to read syntax, and allows programmers to use fewer lines of code than would be possible in languages such as assembly, C, or Java.

The Python programming language actually started as a scripting language for Linux. Python programs are similar to shell scripts in that the files contain a series of commands that the computer executes from top to bottom.

Compare a "hello world" program written in C to the same program written in Python:

Unlike C programs, Python programs don't need to be compiled before running them. However, you will need to install the Python interpreter on your computer to run them. The Python interpreter is a program that reads Python files and executes the code.

It is possible to run Python programs without the Python interpreter installed though. Programs like Py2exe or Pyinstaller will package your Python code into standalone executable programs.

WHAT CAN A PYTHON PROGRAM DO?

Like shell scripts, Python can automate tasks like batch renaming and moving large amounts of files. It can be used just like a command line with IDLE, Python's REPL (read, eval, print, loop) function. However, there are more useful things you can do with Python. For example, you can use Python to program things like:

- Web applications
- Desktop applications and utilities
- Special GUIs
- Small databases
- 2D games

Python also has a large collection of libraries, which speeds up the development process. There are libraries for everything you can think of – game programming, rendering graphics, GUI interfaces, web frameworks, and scientific computing.

Many (but not all) of the things you can do in C can be done in Python. Python is generally slower at computations than C, but its ease of use makes Python an ideal language for prototyping programs and designing applications that aren't computationally intensive.

HOW TO WRITE AND RUN A PROGRAM IN PYTHON

We'll only cover the basics of writing and executing a Python program here, but a great tutorial covering everything a programmer needs to know about Python is the book Learning Python 5th Ed. (O'Reilly) by Mark Lutz.

INSTALLING AND UPDATING PYTHON

Python 2 and Python 3 come preinstalled on Raspbian operating systems, but to install Python on another Linux OS or to update it, simply run one of these commands at the command prompt:

- sudo aptget install python3

- Installs or updates Python 3.

- sudo aptget install python

- Installs or updates Python 2.

OPENING THE PYTHON REPL

To access the Python REPL (where you can enter Python commands just like the command line) enter python or python3 depending on which version you want to use:

Enter CtrlD to exit the REPL.

WRITING A PYTHON PROGRAM

To demonstrate creating and executing a Python program, we'll make a simple "hello world" program. To begin, open the Nano text editor and create a new file named helloworld.py by entering this at the command prompt:

sudo nano helloworld.py

Enter this code into Nano, then press CtrlX and Y to exit and save the file:

```
1 #!/usr/bin/python
2
3 print "Hello, World!";
4
```

All Python program files will need to be saved with a ".py" extension. You can write the program in any text editor such as Notepad or Notepad++, just be sure to save the file with a ".py" extension.

RUNNING A PYTHON PROGRAM

To run the program without making it executable, navigate to the location where you saved your file, and enter this at the command prompt:

python helloworld.py.

MAKE A PYTHON FILE EXECUTABLE

Making a Python program executable allows you to run the program without entering python before the file name. You can make a file executable by entering this at the command prompt:

chmod +x filename.py

Now to run the program, all you need to enter is:

/filename.py

CHAPTER 9:
TIPS AND TRICKS TO USE RASPBERRY PI3

The following steps should be done by new and experienced Raspberry Pi users and will improve the security of your system tenfold.

I will discuss how to delete the default Raspberry Pi 'pi' user as well as changing the password for any other users you create. This is a good first step because if a hacker identify's that your system is running the Rasbian distro then one can assume that there is a user called 'pi' on the system and can begin trying to crack that users password. Deleting the default 'pi' user and creating a new Raspberry Pi username and password will make it much harder to gain access to your system.

I will also be discussing about installing Fail2Ban which will block hackers from bruteforcing your username and password. This is good because it will block the hackers IP Address if they fail to login to your system and they will be unable to perform an unlimited number of username and passwords trying to gain access to your system. Another item that I will be discussing is setting up unique SSH keys, this will allow only clients that have the correct keys that you generated to login to your Raspberry Pi. This is one of the most secure ways of logging into your Raspberry Pi because only computers that you give the generated key file will be able to login and anyone who doesn't have the key file will be blocked.

The final security tip and trick I will show you will be how to setup automated security updates. This is great if you are using your Raspberry Pi as a server and don't access it often. All Raspbian security updates will be downloaded and applied in the background so you know you are running the latest and most secure software.

OBJECTIVE

To learn about and perform basic security steps on our Raspberry Pi to improve our overall security on the Raspberry Pi system

MATERIAL

You will need the following:

- Raspberry Pi

- 8GB Micro SD Card

- 2.5A Power Supply

- Raspbian OS (I will assume you are running Raspbian although this tutorial will apply to any Debian based Linux distro)

1. REMOVE THE DEFAULT 'PI' USER FROM YOUR RASPBER-RY PI

The first Raspberry Pi tip and trick I will be showing you is removing the default 'pi' user from your Raspberry Pi. You will first need to login to the 'pi' user and create your new user. I will be creating a user with the username 'dayz' in my example. After that we will be able to delete the 'pi' user.

Go ahead and open a terminal window or SSH into your Raspberry Pi and run the following command to create your new user (Use the sudo command to run the command as a root user):

1 sudo adduser dayz

You will be asked to enter a password for your new user, enter in the new password and then hit Enter and confirm your password by typing it again. It will ask you to enter the Full Name of this user as well as other information like a Phone number. You can just hit Enter to leave these values blank or you can fill them out.

Once you get the 'Is this information correct [Y/n]' screen you can type Y and then hit Enter.

Now that you created your new user you can log in to your new user with the password you created earlier and we can delete the default 'pi' user. Login to your newly created user and type the following command (Use the sudo command to run the command as root):

1 sudo userdel r pi

Note: The r flag will remove the home folder for the 'pi' user. Be sure to save any files in this folder if you have anything important in them. You can also remove the 'r' flag if you want to keep the home folder.

2. CHANGE THE DEFAULT RASPBERRY PI USER 'PI' PASS-WORD

I highly suggest to remove the 'pi' user if you can but if for any reason you do not want to or you can't then the next best thing to do would be to change the password.

Login to the Raspberry Pi with your 'pi' user and open a terminal window and type the following command to change your password:

1 passwd

You will be prompted to enter in your current password followed by the new password. I suggest using a strong password that you can remember or using a password generator and writing you password down if you will not be logging into the system often.

Once your password is changed you will get the following message:

1 passwd: password updated successfully

Your password change will take effect immediately.

3. INSTALL FAIL2BAN TO BAN BRUTEFORCE ATTEMPTS ON OUR RASPBERRY PI

Fail2Ban is very easy to install and setup and will drastically improve security on your Raspberry Pi. Fail2Ban works by monitoring your logs for failures and depending on the settings you setup it will ban or timeout an IP Address for a certain amount of time if it fails to login to your server. It is a great tool and a must have tool to protect your from bruteforce attacks. If you want to find out more information about Fail2Ban check out my article here. It goes into more detail as to what exactly we will be doing and more configuration options.

Lets install Fail2Ban by typing the following commands after opening a terminal window or logging in through SSH:

1 sudo aptget update

2 sudo aptget install fail2ban

The initial settings for Fail2Ban are located at '/etc/fail2ban/jail.conf'. You can see all the default settings for many services that you are being protected against. However do not edit any of these settings in your '/etc/fail2ban/jail.conf' file. You will want to edit the '/etc/fail2ban/jail.local' file and add your configurations there.

Lets edit our SSH Fail2Ban configurations. Open up the '/etc/fail2ban/jail.local' file with the following command:

1 sudo nano /etc/fail2ban/jail.local

Your jail.local file should be empty. Lets add the following settings:

1 [ssh]

2

3 enabled = true

4 port = ssh

5 filter = sshd

6 logpath = /var/log/auth.log

7 bantime = 900

8 banaction = iptablesallports

9 findtime = 900

10 maxretry = 3

After pasting the settings hit CTRL+X and then Y to save the configuration file.

Restart Fail2Ban with the following command to make your configuration settings live:

sudo service fail2ban restart

At this point Fail2Ban is configured and your server will be protected from bruteforce attacks however all bans will be cleared upon restarting Fail2Ban or rebooting the server. If you manage to ban yourself you can simply restart your Raspberry Pi.

4. PERFORM SECURITY UPDATES AUTOMATICALLY ON THE RASPBERRY PI

Keeping up with security on your Raspberry Pi will require some maintenance and having to check and apply for security upgrades periodically. This can be troublesome if you are using your Raspberry Pi as a server and don't normally access it on a regular basis. There is a solution. You can setup a cron schedule to check for and perform updates using the 'aptget update' and 'aptget upgrade' commands but these command will upgrade all your software too. This can be an issue because some updated software can break other programs running in the background. Since we are focusing on easy security tips and tricks we will be installing 'unattendedupgrades'.

Lets install unattendedupgrades with the following command:

1 sudo aptget install unattendedupgrades

Once the unattendedupgrades package is installed we will want to configure it. There are a few configurations we can perform. Type the following command to edit the configuration file for unateendedupgrades:

1 sudo nano /etc/apt/apt.conf.d/50unattendedupgrades

The packages that we want to upgrade are located in between UnattendedUpgrade::OriginsPattern { } in the configuration file. You will either need to uncomment the Raspbian line or add the following line to perform only Raspbian Jessie Security updates:

1 "o=Raspbian,n=jessie,l=RaspbianSecurity";

Your UnattendedUpgrade::OriginsPattern { } should look something similar to this:

```
1 UnattendedUpgrade::OriginsPattern {

2 // Codename based matching:

3 // This will follow the migration of a release through different

4 // archives (e.g. from testing to stable and later oldstable).

5 "o=Raspbian,n=jessie,l=RaspbianSecurity";

6

7 // Archive or Suite based matching:

8 // Note that this will silently match a different release after

9 // migration to the specified archive (e.g. testing becomes the

10 // new stable).

11 // "o=Raspbian,a=stable";

12

13 };
```

There are a few other configurations you can set like the time to perform the updates as well as sending you an email but this is just the basic setup tips and tricks tutorial. Now your Raspberry Pi will perform automatic security updates daily.

5. SETUP SSH KEY PAIRING TO LOGIN TO YOUR RASPBERRY PI

SSH Keys allow you to login to your server without a password and the client and server will use these keys to authenticate the client allowing it access. This is safer because it prevents bruteforce attacks. You can however add a passphrase to your key, meaning that you would need to have a private key as well as a passphrase to connect to the server. Adding a passphrase would really lockdown our server and make it virtually impossible to connect into without the SSH key and passphrase.

Setting up SSH Keys will require you to set them up on your main computer (client) that you will be accessing the Raspberry Pi from. The Raspberry Pi in this scenario will be your server. What will happen is you will generate the SSH keys on your client and then transfer the key to the server so that way only that client will be able to access the server with those keys. Setting up SSH keys is not difficult but it is a lot more detail then I can explain in a few paragraphs. You can check out my full article on SSH keys here.

Note

Those are 5 basic Raspberry Pi security tips and tricks that every user must do. These should only take a few minutes to perform and should be done on every Raspberry Pi setup. Having so many devices being connected to the internet now really increases the risks of your network and personal information. These tips and tricks may not stop a hacker from gaining access into your system but it definitely stops hackers who are simply looking for easy ways into your network.

CHAPTER 10: CREATING A CLASSIC GAME EMULATOR

Raspberry Pi is a singleboard, supersimple computer that can do a surprising amount. It costs $35, though that only gets you the computer itself — there's no power supply, no onboard storage, no keyboard or mouse or way to connect to a monitor. But for $35 you get a computer with a 1.2 GHz processor and 1 GB of RAM, about the same specs as an iPhone 5 or some Chromebooks. (It's powerful enough you could reasonably, with some work and compromises, use a Pi as your main work machine.)

Running an emulator, a program designed to let a operating system behave like another one, is actually one of the more basic things you can do with a Pi. People have strung multiple Pis together to form a supercomputer, created working weather stations with them, and sent them up in weather balloons to take photos from the edge of the Earth's atmosphere. Emulating a PlayStation 1 on it is comparatively trivial.

Here's everything I needed to do it.

A quick rundown of what everything is, and how much it cost.

1: 10foot Micro USB cord from Anker ($6.99), mainly so I could use a wired controller from a comfortable distance from the screen

2: SB Components Clear Case for Raspberry Pi 3 ($5.58)

3: Raspberry Pi 3 Model B Board ($35) and LoveRPi Performance Heatsink Set for Raspberry Pi 3 ($4.99).

4: PS4 DualShock Controller ($46.99). I should note I already owned one of these, and any USB controller will work here, so any Xbox 360, Xbox One, or PS3 controller will all work fine. If you don't have any of those, these Baigeda Game Controllers are $12.49.

5: AmazonBasics 3foot HDMI Cable ($5.99)

6: SanDisk 16GB MicroSDHC Card with Adapter ($5.95)

7: Keten Raspberry Pi 3 Power Supply ($8.99)

8: A 2001era USB EZ Keyboard meant for FinalCut Pro that my father had in the back of a closet ($??). If you can't lay hands on a USB keyboard, you can get this Gear Head USB keyboard for $5.99.

Not Pictured: A 19inch Panasonic CRT TV in the guest room at my parent's place and a MacBook Pro I used to download some software and write to the microSD card.

All in all, I spent $73.49 on everything. If I didn't have a keyboard or game controller I could use, I would have spent $91.97. And I should say, I went about this slightly stupidly; there are bundles that include a lot of this stuff for comparable prices. This Vilros Raspberry Pi 3 Basic Starter Kit, for example, includes a Pi 3, a case, a power supply, and two heat sinks for $49.99, when I paid $54.56 for essentially the same parts. I also could have cannibalized one of the many HDMI cables I have, and just used the micro USB cord that came with my PlayStation 4 instead of buying a new one. If you have any of these things, you could easily get away with spending under $60, and maybe even just $50 for the basic starter kit if you also have a microSD card lying around.

After snapping the case around the Pi board, I hooked it up to a TV, controller, and power supply. If you've ever set up any videogame console or even, like, a Roku box, all of this should be second nature: The HDMI cable goes into the TV; then you hook up power supply to an outlet, and plug the controller into one of the four USB slots provided.

After that, it was time to load up an emulator. Luckily, there's a program made for just this purpose: RetroPie. Partly a free program and partly a bundle of a lot of other emulator and controller programs already floating around, it's remarkably easy to get set up and running, and supports emulation on over 50 systems, everything from old Amiga games to MAME, which lets you run many old arcade cabinet titles.

First download RetroPie, Once you've downloaded the program, you'll need to write it to your microSD card. If you're using a PC, use a program like Win32DiskImager. If you're using a Mac, use something like Apple Pi Baker. If you're using Linux, there is no way in hell you need help doing any of this.

After that, remove the the microSD from the adapter and slot the card into your Pi (the microSD card will function essentially as your Pi's solidstate hard drive). After a moment, you'll see a very oldschoollooking DOS screen pop up as RetroPie boots itself up. From there, you'll have a pretty slick frontend that will do the majority of the work for you. You'll need to map the buttons on your controller in RetroPie, and then you'll be able to start looking around.

Next, you'll want to plug in your USB keyboard, because the next thing you want to do is load in some ROMs. To do that, you'll want to get the Pi's onboard WiFi up and running. Navigate the main config menu over to "Configure WiFi," and select that. You'll need to find your WiFi network and type in the password, and since there's no default keyboard you can use with a controller setup, you'll need a keyboard here. (You'll want to keep the keyboard handy if you want to monkey around in more advanced settings as well.)

Once WiFi is up and running, you can transfer over ROMs, which are basically the files of each individual game. Here is where I should say: ROMs are sometimes described as being in a "legal gray area," but in reality downloading a ROM is in violation of the DMCA and existing copyright laws. Download ROMs at your own risk, and you're gonna have to find them on your own. Best of luck.

But, if you do happen to have ROMs around, you'll want to transfer them over. You can load them in via a USB stick, but that's actually clunkier than just transferring them over your WiFi network. To transfer files, you'll need to use a SFTP (SSH File Transfer Protocol) program. WinSCP is the most popular option for Windows users, and on the Mac most people use Cyberduck.

Once you have those programs running, you'll be able to set up direct file transfers to your Pi. To do this, you'll need the Pi's username and password. By default, the username is "pi" and the password is "raspberry" (with no quotes around either).

Whew! This may seem like a lot, but you're pretty much at the finish line. Drop your ROM files from your computer into the correct emulator system folder (so, for instance, Nintendo games should go in the file named "nes"). You'll see the game appear instantly, usually, though I found I had to reset RetroPie once or twice to get it to recognize a new game.

From there, scroll to the system you want to play, find the game you want to boot up, and you're done. While this may seem like a lot of steps, in reality it's just downloading various programs and getting them up and running.

CHAPTER 11:
BUILDING A STREAMING PROGRAM FOR YOUR MEDIA WITH A RASPBERRY PI3

One of the most popular uses for the lowcost Raspberry Pi computers is as a media center. Indeed, it doesn't matter whether you're using a Model A, a Raspberry Pi Zero, or a Raspberry Pi 3 – while the later model will naturally offer superior performance, the fact is that all of the devices can deliver you compact, affordable, lowpower, media center solution.

But which media center application should you install on your Raspberry Pi's SD card? Several options are on offer, and we're going to walk you through them now, looking at the features, advantages, and disadvantages of each.

READYMEDIA (MINIDLNA)

Formerly known as MiniDLNA, ReadyMedia requires installing on a standard Raspberry Pi operating system, such as Raspbian Jessie. Start by mounting the disk drive(s) with the media data on, and then use the standard installation command:

sudo aptget install minidlna

Once installed, this simple tool is compatible with DLNA/UPnPAV, which means that any DLNAcompatible device on the same network should be able to detect your Pi and play media from it.

Fast, lightweight and easily configurable, ReadyMedia is the option to choose if you just want to stream your media and have no interest in indexing it.

Kodi/OpenElec

Perhaps the most recognized name in this list, Kodi — formerly XBMC — is available for the Raspberry Pi. Various options are available for this. Among them are writing a full Kodibased distro to SD card and manual installation using:

sudo aptget install kodi

Such distros include OpenElec, OSMC and XBian. You may already know that OpenElec is available on NOOBs for easy installation.

But wait a minute. Aren't the Kodibased media servers actually media centers? Well, they're actually both, which is how they come to be in this list. While you might use these distros (or manually install Kodi) as a media center/HTPC solution on a Raspberry Pi, the provision of DLNA/UPnP means that Kodi (and its forks) can be used as a media server.

If you're already using OpenElec, OSMX, XBian, etc., then you don't need a media server as you already have one. Simply open Settings > Services > UPnP and enable Share video and music libraries through UPnP. You'll then have the ability to stream content from your Kodibased system. It's simple, but demands that you have already set up the media center software and attached the various hard disk drives that store your media.

OpenMediaVault

Admittedly closer to a NAS than a media server, OpenMediaVault is the current smart choice for Pi owners wishing to make their media files (and documents and other data) available to them from any device on the same network.

Setup is straightforward, if lengthy, but you may run into initial problems mounting any hard disk drives that you have connected to your Pi. This should be quickly overcome, however, enabling you to configure the system correctly. Among the features with OMV are support for a UPS (uninterruptible power supplies) and statistics pages to assist in system monitoring. There is also EXT3/EXT4/XFS/ JFS filesystem support and RAID can be set up for HDD mirroring. SSH, FTP, TFTP, SMB and RSync are all supported for direct connection to your OMV device, although you will typically access it via your web browser, by opening the IP address.

Various plugins are also available for OMV, such as a Bittorrent client. You can try a demo version of the console on the OMV website.

PLEX MEDIA SERVER

If you prefer to simply stream from a desktop or dedicated media server to your Raspberry Pi, seek out Plex. A popular name in home media streaming, Plex can be used to stream content to all manner of devices, even the Google Chromecast.

Using Plex Media Server with your Raspberry Pi requires you to first download the RasPlex client installer to your Windows, Mac or Linux PC and write the software to an SD card compatible with your Pi.

Beyond the Raspberry Pi, you'll be able to enjoy media streamed via Plex on a wide selection of devices, as Plex is perhaps the widestused of all media server applications. Mobile apps are available for Android, iOS and Windows 10 Mobile, while media streamers such as Apple TV, Amazon Fire TV and many Smart TVs also have Plex clients. There are even clients for Xbox One and PlayStation 4, as well as Windows, and Mac OS X, while various thirdparty builds are available for Linux.

Note that Plex demands that your files are named in a particular format if it is to pull the appropriate metadata from the Web. This support page from the Plex website explains file organization and naming.

As things stand, Plex should be your first choice of media server, and the RasPlex client is as good as the mainstream version. For the best results, however, make sure you're using a Raspberry Pi 2 or Raspberry Pi 3.

CHAPTER 12:
A PERSONAL ASSITANTS MADE
WITH RASPBERRY PI3

S ometime ago, I was struck by the idea that the intercom would be ideal in combination with the pi, to build a voice controlled device.

Because of the intercom, the idea came that it would be funny to use the intercom for what it was intended: contacting your personal assistant to get information or to give him/her a task. The only difference is that this intercom isn't connected to its other half but to the raspberry pi. And that there is no real person on the other side, but a smart little computer that can do a lot of the same things as that real person.

In this CHAPTER, I'll show you:

- how to connect the pi to the intercom

- how to set up the pi

- how to install the voicecontrole software

- how to add a speech script that will return the output of your own scripts as speech

STEP 1: WHAT DO YOU NEED FOR THIS PROJECT?

For this project we need:

- A Raspberry pi model B with Raspian Wheezy installed.

- A USB WIFI adaptor: I used a Delock Nano Stick 150MB/s. It cost about $18

- A USB soundcard: it cost $3.21 at Deal Extreme.

- A small 5V amplifier: I used a PAM8403 board. It cost $5.64 at Deal Extreme.

- A 5V power supply: at least 2A.

- A 5V DPDT relais: DPDT means Double Pole Double Throw. The relais is able to switch two different signals between two different outputs.

- A tiny piece of vero board

- Some wires

- A USB keyboard and mouse + a tv with HDMI or video in connection for installing everything on the Pi

STEP 2: INSTALLING THE WIFI.

In this step , I'll show you how to connect to the internet via the raspberry desktop. But before you do anything, update your raspberry. Make sure that your Pi is connected to the internet via a cable.

To update, startup the raspberry and on the desktop, open the terminal. Enter the following commands in the terminal.

sudo aptget upgrade

Once this is done shut down the raspberry:

sudo poweroff

Now insert the USB WIFI adaptor and turn on the power again.

On the desktop, double click the Wifi Config Icon. A window will open.

Click the scanbutton which will again open a new window.

In that window, select your SSID by doubleclicking it.

A window appears and you should add the password where it says PSK. Then click Add.

You will be back in the first window. There you can see the status of the connection at the IP.

You should now have a Wifi connection.

You can shut the Pi down for now.

STEP 3: SETTING UP THE HARDWARE.

Show All 13 Items

Inside the intercom, there is not enough space to hide everything, when the whole setup is done with jacks to connect the audio. So to address this problem, I opened the plastic case of the USB sound card and desoldered the connectors. Then I soldered wires to the spots where the connectors were. The connection of these wires will be discussed later in this step.

Most intercoms use the speaker as microphone. So this means that we have to devise a method to connect the same speaker to the output and the microphone input of the USB sound card. There is a push button in the front that was used originally to switch between listen and speak, so that can be of use to us.

It has to be said that I didn't want to change anything on the outside of the intercom because it's such a nice thing in great condition. Drilling holes in it was no option. Otherwise I could simply have added a DPDT switch to switch between input and output. So I had to find the next simplest method.

This is where the 5V DPDT relais comes in. We can use the push button of the intercom to switch it. To do this, we connect 5V to the push button and the second wire of the button goes to one side of the relay coil. The other side of the coil goes directly to ground. So when you press the button, the coil is activated and the relay switches. It is good practice to add a diode in the opposite direction over the 2 pins of the coil.

The centerpins of the DPDT relays are connected to the + and of the speaker. The NO (Normally Open) pins are connected to the microphone input of the USB soundcard. The NC (Normally Closed) pins need to be connected to the output of the soundcard. But the signal of that output is not loud enough for the speaker so we need to put an amplifier between them.

The Amplifier I used, is quite simple to hook up. Everything is clearly marked on the PCB. Connect the 5V pin to 5V and the GND pin to GND and you have power. Then connect the output and GND from the soundcard to Rin and GND and connect R+ and R to the NC pins of the relay.

When this is done, everything can be placed into the case. Connect the soundcard to the pi.

It is not a very good idea to try to power everything from the raspberry pi. So I found a 5V 3A wall adaptor to power this project. I did cut of the connector and connected everything inside to it. To do so I had to cut a USB cord. That allowed me to connect to the pi without having to desolder the onboard USB connector.

When everything is hooked up this way, your hardware is set up and the case can be closed.

STEP 4: SETTING UP THE USB SOUND CARD.

The raspberry pi needs a little bit of preparation to use a USB soundcard. There is a very good adafruit tutorial for this.

I'll give you the short version here. My soundcard was a CM109 version so the only thing I had to do was to open the alsa config file:

sudo nano /etc/modprobe.d/alsabase.conf

And change:

options sndusbaudio index=2

into:

options sndusbaudio index=0

And then reboot the pi:

sudo reboot

STEP 5: SETTING UP THE VOICECOMMAND SOFTWARE.

I used Steven Hicksons voice command software. If you are looking for voice command software for your pi, stop looking and use this one. It is by far the easiest to setup and to use. It is also very well documented and it is quite reliable.

You can download it from his website and there are also some videos there that show you how you can set it up.

The voicecommand software comes as a part of a whole suite of media related applications for the pi. I only installed the voicecommand software, but if you like to use more of them for your project, then feel free to install them.

When the software is installed, you can enter the following command:

voicecommand s

It will start an automatic setup process that guides you stepbystep through the setup of your device.

When this is done, you can enter:

voicecommand e

This will open the config file and allow you to set the commando's and the related actions.

It has to be entered in the following format:

command==action

The command system is pretty simple. When you set the command to play, it will only react when you say nothing else but 'play'. When you set it to play music it will only react to 'play music' and not to 'play' or 'play chess'. But when you set it to ~play it will react to any sentence that contains 'play'.

The action can be any executable command.

When you are done editing the config file, save it and everything is ready.

To run the software just enter:

voicecommand c

and enjoy your personal assistant. The good lady will now listen to your commands and perform the appropriate task. When she doesn't find a matching task to a command you gave, she will look it up on Google and she will try to give you a satisfying answer. You can finish the project now but in the next steps I will show you how to get more out of it.

STEP 6: MAKE IT RUN ON STARTUP.

It is ofcourse nice if the voicecommand starts to work on start up. To do this we need to add a little script.

In the home directory (home/pi), open the .config directory

cd .config

then create a new directory:

mkdir autostart go into that directory:

cd autostart and in that directory open a new file in nano:

sudo nano voicecommand.desktop

Write the following code in the file:

[Desktop Entry]

Type=Application

Name=Voicecommand

Exec=voicecommand c

StartupNotify=false

Save the file and reboot the Pi.

STEP 7: GIVE YOUR OWN APPS A VOICE.

It's all very nice that the device is able to start programs and return info from the internet, but sometimes you want to receive very specific data in a certain way. For instance the weather forecast for your area. One thing you can do(as I did) is to write your own python script that gets the data from the internet, filters out the data you want and returns it in a way that makes sense. The only problem is that those scripts return that data as written text and not as speech. So we need an extra script to do that for us.

I found a very nice script on Oscar Liang's blog. Just like voicecommand, it uses Google speech service to 'translate' the text into speech.

The first one you need is the text2speech.sh script. (I'll copy it here but all credits go to Oscar Liang) copy it into nano or the text editor on the graphic desktop

```
#!/bin/bash

INPUT=$*

STRINGNUM=0

ary=($INPUT)

for key in "${!ary[@]}"

do

SHORTTMP[$STRINGNUM]="${SHORTTMP[$STRINGNUM]} ${ary[$key]}"

LENGTH=$(echo ${#SHORTTMP[$STRINGNUM]})


if [[ "$LENGTH" lt "100" ]]; then


SHORT[$STRINGNUM]=${SHORTTMP[$STRINGNUM]}

else

STRINGNUM=$(($STRINGNUM+1))

SHORTTMP[$STRINGNUM]="${ary[$key]}"

SHORT[$STRINGNUM]="${ary[$key]}"

fi

done
```

```
for key in "${!SHORT[@]}"

do

say() { local IFS=+;/usr/bin/mplayer ao alsa reallyquiet noconsolecontrols
"http://translate.google.com/translate_tts?tl=en&q=${SHORT[$key]}";
}

say $*

done
```

Once you have saved this script, make it executable with:

chmod +x text2speech.sh

This script will be reusable for all applications that need conversion to speech.

The only thing we need now are scripts that run the python script and pump the output into thetext2speech script. We'll need one of these scripts for each python script.

#!/bin/bash

ANSWER=$(python yourpythonscriptname.py)

./text2speech.sh $ANSWER

Save this as whateveryoulike.sh and make it executable.

now you can enter this script into the config file of voicecommand and it will return speech whenever the right command is entered.

CHAPTER 13:
A WIRELESS ACCESS POINT

The Raspberry Pi can be used as a wireless access point, running a standalone network. This can be done using the inbuilt wireless features of the Raspberry Pi 3 or Raspberry Pi Zero W, or by using a suitable USB wireless dongle that supports access points.

Note that this documentation was tested on a Raspberry Pi 3, and it is possible that some USB dongles may need slight changes to their settings. If you are having trouble with a USB wireless dongle, please check the forums.

To add a Raspberry Pibased access point to an existing network, see this section.

In order to work as an access point, the Raspberry Pi will need to have access point software installed, along with DHCP server software to provide connecting devices with a network address. Ensure that your Raspberry Pi is using an uptodate version of Raspbian (dated 2017 or later).

Use the following to update your Raspbian installation:

sudo aptget update

sudo aptget distupgrade

Install all the required software in one go with this command:

sudo aptget install dnsmasq hostapd

Since the configuration files are not ready yet, turn the new software off as follows:

sudo systemctl stop dnsmasq

sudo systemctl stop hostapd

CONFIGURING A STATIC IP

We are configuring a standalone network to act as a server, so the Raspberry Pi needs to have a static IP address assigned to the wireless port. This documentation assumes that we are using the standard 192.168.x.x IP addresses for our wireless network, so we will assign the server the IP address 192.168.0.1. It is also assumed that the wireless device being used is wlan0.

First, the standard interface handling for wlan0 needs to be disabled. Normally the dhcpcd daemon (DHCP client) will search the network for a DHCP server to assign a IP address to wlan0. This is disabled by editing the configuration file:

sudo nano /etc/dhcpcd.conf

Add denyinterfaces wlan0 to the end of the file (but above any other added interface lines) and save the file.

To configure the static IP address, edit the interfaces configuration file with:

sudo nano /etc/network/interfaces

Find the wlan0 section and edit it so that it looks like the following:

allowhotplug wlan0

iface wlan0 inet static

> *address 192.168.0.1*

> *netmask 255.255.255.0*

> *network 192.168.0.0*

Now restart the dhcpcd daemon and set up the new wlan0 configuration:

sudo service dhcpcd restart

sudo ifdown wlan0

sudo ifup wlan0

CONFIGURING THE DHCP SERVER (DNSMASQ)

The DHCP service is provided by dnsmasq. By default, the configuration file contains a lot of information that is not needed, and it is easier to start from scratch. Rename this configuration file, and edit a new one:

sudo mv /etc/dnsmasq.conf /etc/dnsmasq.conf.orig

sudo nano /etc/dnsmasq.conf

Type or copy the following information into the dnsmasq configuration file and save it:

interface=wlan0   # Use the require wireless interface usually wlan0

dhcprange=192.168.0.2,192.168.0.20,255.255.255.0,24h

So for wlan0, we are going to provide IP addresses between 192.168.0.2 and 192.168.0.20, with a lease time of 24 hours. If you are providing DHCP services for other network devices (e.g. eth0), you could add more sections with the appropriate interface header, with the range of addresses you intend to provide to that interface.

There are many more options for dnsmasq; see the dnsmasq documentation for more details.

CONFIGURING THE ACCESS POINT HOST SOFTWARE (HOSTAPD)

You need to edit the hostapd configuration file, located at /etc/hostapd/hostapd. conf, to add the various parameters for your wireless network. After initial install, this will be a new/empty file.

sudo nano /etc/hostapd/hostapd.conf

Add the information below to the configuration file. This configuration assumes we are using channel 7, with a network name of NameOfNetwork, and a password AardvarkBadgerHedgehog. Note that the name and password should not have quotes around them.

```
interface=wlan0
driver=nl80211
ssid=NameOfNetwork
hw_mode=g
channel=7
wmm_enabled=0
macaddr_acl=0
auth_algs=1
ignore_broadcast_ssid=0
wpa=2
wpa_passphrase=AardvarkBadgerHedgehog
wpa_key_mgmt=WPAPSK
wpa_pairwise=TKIP
rsn_pairwise=CCMP
```

We now need to tell the system where to find this configuration file.

```
sudo nano /etc/default/hostapd
```

Find the line with #DAEMON_CONF, and replace it with this:

```
DAEMON_CONF="/etc/hostapd/hostapd.conf"
```

START IT UP

Now start up the remaining services:

sudo service hostapd start

sudo service dnsmasq start

Using a wireless device, search for networks. The network SSID you specified in the hostapd configuration should now be present, and it should be accessible with the specified password.

If SSH is enabled on the Raspberry Pi access point, it should be possible to connect to it from another Linux box (or a system with SSH connectivity present) as follows, assuming the pi account is present:

ssh pi@192.168.0.1

By this point, the Raspberry Pi is acting as an access point, and other devices can associate with it. Associated devices can access the Raspberry Pi access point via its IP address for operations such as rsync, scp, or ssh.

USING THE RASPBERRY PI3 AS AN ACCESS POINT TO SHARE AN INTERNET CONNECTION

One common use of the Raspberry Pi as an access point is to provide wireless connections to a wired Ethernet connection, so that anyone logged into the access point can access the internet, providing of course that the wired Ethernet on the Pi can connect to the internet via some sort of router.

To do this, a 'bridge' needs to put in place between the wireless device and the Ethernet device on the access point Raspberry Pi. This bridge will pass all traffic between the two interfaces. Install the following packages to enable the access point setup and bridging.

sudo aptget install hostapd bridgeutils

Since the configuration files are not ready yet, turn the new software off as follows:

sudo systemctl stop hostapd

Bridging creates a higherlevel construct over the two ports being bridged. It is the bridge that is the network device, so we need to stop the eth0 and wlan0 ports being allocated IP addresses by the DHCP client on the Raspberry Pi.

sudo nano /etc/dhcpcd.conf

Add denyinterfaces wlan0 and denyinterfaces eth0 to the end of the file (but above any other added interface lines) and save the file.

Add a new bridge, which in this case is called br0.

sudo brctl addbr br0

Connect the network ports. In this case, connect eth0 to wlan0.

sudo brctl addif br0 eth0 wlan0

Now the interfaces file needs to be edited to adjust the various devices to work with bridging. sudo nano /etc/network/interfaces make the following edits.

Change the wlan entry to manual if it not already so, and remove any other entries e.g. any static address.

> *allowhotplug wlan0*
>
> *iface wlan0 inet manual*
>
> *Add the bridging information at the end of the file.*
>
> *# Bridge setup*
>
> *auto br0*
>
> *iface br0 inet dhcp*
>
> *bridge_ports eth0 wlan0*

The access point setup is almost the same as that shown in the previous section. Follow the instructions above to set up the hostapd.conf file, but add bridge=br0 below the interface=wlan0 line, and remove or comment out the driver line.

> *interface=wlan0*
>
> *bridge=br0*
>
> *#driver=nl80211*
>
> *...*

Now reboot the Raspberry Pi3.

There should now be a functioning bridge between the wireless LAN and the Ethernet connection on the Raspberry Pi, and any device associated with the Raspberry Pi access point will act as if it is connected to the access point's wired Ethernet.

The ifconfig command will show the bridge, which will have been allocated an IP address via the wired Ethernet's DHCP server. The wlan0 and eth0 no longer have IP addresses, as they are now controlled by the bridge. It is possible to use a static IP address for the bridge if required, but generally, if the Raspberry Pi access point is connected to a ADSL router, the DHCP address will be fine.

CONCLUSION

The Raspberry Pi is a powerful little beast and a great platform for building lowcost, but highly capable, embedded systems. The interfaces built into its GPIO connector make it easy to bolt on modules using simple lowcost electronics and a bit of configuration to create very functional and flexible systems. The inclusion of a dedicated camera interface and networking interfaces give you everything you could possible need for an Internetconnected home security system.

I've covered a lot of topics in this book, and I could have gone on and on, but I hope that what I have presented has been done in a structured and methodical way, and has given you the tools and techniques to carry on this journey so that you are able to create the perfect home security system for your needs.

As a systems guy who has to work with many different technologies and disciplines on a daytoday basis, I just want to leave you with the following thoughts to consider, if you choose to build upon the system we've put together in this book, which, of course, I hope you will.

THANKS FOR READING!!!